DEREK THE FLYING DODO

THE NEXT BIG ADVENTURE

VANEE APOOLINGUM

ILLUSTRATED BY DANIEL McCLOSKEY

ISBN 978-1-7384585-2-3 (ebook)
ISBN 978-1-7384585-3-0 (paperback)

Published in 2023 by Vara Ink Books

For Aiden, Alexander and Richard
Thank you for
all the adventures

For my Mum
With love and thanks

CHAPTER 1

Face dripping with sweat and legs aching like he had run a thousand marathons, Derek dragged his tired body to the top of the rocky mountain. He had finally managed to escape the vicious pack of wolves and bravely rescued his best friend Aaron, who was being held captive by them.

"What an incredible, daring adventure that was!" shouted Derek elatedly.

Suddenly, in the distance, he could hear someone calling his name, "Derek, wake up Derek. Come on, it's time to get up!" As Derek slowly opened his tired eyes, he could see Mummy Dodo standing over him with her usual beaming morning smile.

"Oh no, not another dream of an adventure. This one felt so real," sighed

Derek as he drooped his head low and a little tear trickled down his beautiful blue feathers.

He felt an instant sadness and clutched Mummy Dodo tightly for some much-needed comfort.

As some of you may know, dodos can't fly, but Derek was rather unique. After wishing on a shooting star, Derek got his wish of being able to fly. He then went on an adventure of a lifetime where he met his best friend Aaron, encountered dancing peacocks and mean monkeys, and discovered a truly magnificent rainbow waterfall. However, all of that seemed to be a distant memory now.

"I do love it here in the jungle, but doing the same thing every day can get very boring," sighed Derek.

Mummy Dodo knew exactly what to say to Derek and, with an encouraging smile, told him, "Well, maybe if the

adventure is not coming to you, you need to go and get it instead."

Upon hearing this, Derek leapt from his bed and gave Mummy Dodo the biggest hug he could give. "I think it is high time for me to be brave again and leave the comfort of the jungle and go in search of some new adventures," announced Derek excitedly to Mummy Dodo.

The very next morning, as the scorching sun pushed the moon out of the way, Derek woke up with a spring in his step, ready to fly off in search of an exciting new adventure. He hugged Mummy Dodo, Daddy Dodo and Grandad Dodo as tightly as he could and promised to come back to them safe and sound. Then, without wasting another minute, Derek started flying over the luscious, emerald-green jungle and soared higher and higher in the direction of the pristine sandy beach where his best friend Aaron lived.

CHAPTER 2

As Derek touched down in front of Aaron's chocolate-brown hut, he suddenly felt some little raindrops on his delicate feathers. He looked up at the sky, which was now a slate grey instead of its usual aquamarine blue. He knew what was coming. A storm! However, he was so desperate for a new adventure that he was not going to let anything get in his way.

He knocked on Aaron's door, his heart beating with exhilaration at the anticipation of seeing his best friend and fellow adventurer again. Seconds later, the door burst open, and there stood Aaron, grinning from ear to ear at the sight of Derek.

Derek did not waste any time in speaking to his friend about his plans, exclaiming enthusiastically, "Hi Aaron, I have been thinking it's the perfect time

that we set off on another adventure around the island!"

Aaron was in complete agreement with his friend but was a bit more cautious than Derek.

"I would love to join you, but I think the storm is getting worse and could turn into a cyclone. It will be best if we wait until it blows over," said Aaron with great disappointment in his voice.

Both Aaron and Derek looked up at the now charcoal-grey sky, and those little raindrops had now turned into a heavy downpour accompanied by very strong winds. Deep down, Derek knew that his friend was right, but his thirst for adventure was too strong, and he could not wait any longer to fly off.

He convinced Aaron that he was skilled at flying now and that they would be safe, even in this unpredictable weather. Aaron half-heartedly agreed, as he did not want

to disappoint his best friend, especially after he had come such a long way to see him. Reluctantly, Aaron climbed onto Derek's back and clutched onto his neck as tightly as a child holding on to their favourite teddy.

CHAPTER 3

Feeling a mixture of fear and trepidation, both friends soared through the stormy sky, fully aware that it was certainly not the right decision to make.

"Derek, I think we should really find somewhere to land, the cyclone is not stopping anytime soon," said Aaron in a shaky voice.

However, the wind and the rain were so loud that Derek could not hear his friend and the tremendous amount of fear that accompanied his statement. The lightning flashed in the midnight black sky and was promptly followed by the loudest thunder the island had ever heard. It was like the roar of a thousand lions all at once.

Derek was trying extremely hard to fly straight, but it was becoming more and

more difficult to do. The heavy rain was pelting down harder than ever, and in the process made it tricky for Derek to see what lay ahead. His eyes started to sting from the rain, and it was getting harder for him to flap his wings. Both Derek and the island had become complete prisoners of the deluge that the cyclone was unleashing on them. There was nothing he could do to ease his current predicament except hope that he and Aaron were going to come out of this truly terrifying situation unscathed.

As they flew across a grove of palm trees, those big branches which once upon a time stood tall and proud were now bowing down to the intensity of the weather.

Derek turned around to look at his friend and shouted these words to reassure him, even though he did not quite believe them himself. "Don't worry Aaron, I think we have passed the worst of it, and I am sure the sun will smile

down on us any minute now."

Aaron hoped that his friend was right and gave a quick nod in agreement. However, this optimism was short-lived. Both the rain and heavy winds had now completely obscured Derek's view, and he did not see the very tall coconut tree that was right in front of him. He flew straight into it, knocking down some coconuts in the process. Derek and Aaron fell flat on the ground, and they lay there motionless from the sheer shock of what had just happened to them.

CHAPTER 4

After what felt like an absolute lifetime, Aaron tried to move from the uncomfortable, debris-covered ground he was lying on. His whole body was aching all over, but he had to get up and help Derek, who was in way worse shape than he was.

Aaron carefully dragged his achy limbs to where Derek was still lying and bent down to check on his friend. "Derek, are you okay?" he whispered gently into his ear.

Derek slowly turned around to look at him, and his face was filled with guilt and sadness. "I am sorry I did not listen to you Aaron. We should never have left the beach in this weather," he replied back in a soft and teary voice.

Aaron loved his friend too much to be

upset with him. He was just relieved that Derek was okay and to him that was all that mattered. He gave Derek a gentle hug to let his friend know that all was forgiven and he was not upset with him. Aaron helped Derek get up. However, as he did that, a terrifying realisation dawned on Derek. His left wing was broken! He could not flap it or move it and he was in a lot of discomfort. Both friends were in the middle of a grove of coconut trees, very far away from anywhere they knew. A sudden wave of panic came across them.

How on earth were they going to make it back home?

As the friends stood there alarmed over their current predicament, they heard slow, heavy steps approaching them. By now, the heavy downpour had stopped and only a little drizzle was coming from the sky. The friends turned around to face two of the biggest tortoises they had ever seen. Their rounded, hard rock shells were made up of beautiful chestnut-brown hexagonal plates. They both had long, wrinkly necks, and their tiny eyes stared straight at Aaron and Derek. Their eyes were filled with warmth and kindness, and one of them gently approached the two friends.

"Hi, my name is Tara and this is my brother Toby," she said, pointing to the other tortoise next to her. "Can we both be of any help to you?" she added in a calming and reassuring tone.

Both friends started to relax and quickly related their misadventure to Tara. She listened intently to the whole story and quickly promised that she would help them get back on their way.

She explained to Derek and Aaron that they lived in an underground burrow, not very far from the coconut grove. She then told the friends to hop on their backs and they would take them to their burrow to get Derek's wing fixed. An enormous look of relief swept across Aaron and Derek's

faces and they felt so grateful to have crossed paths with these two giant souls.

They climbed onto the tortoises' backs, which were smooth and firm to the touch, and their new friends carried them slowly to their underground burrow. The burrow was covered with different coloured soil ranging from scarlet red and vibrant purple to a luminous yellow. It was truly a mesmerising sight, like nothing the friends had ever come across before.

CHAPTER 5

As they entered the burrow, they finally got some respite from the dreadful weather that they had been subjected to so far. It was beautiful inside, with lush green foliage everywhere and divinely scented flowers and fruits growing in every corner of the burrow. However, the friends suddenly came to a stop. Right in front of them, sitting on a very ornate throne covered with flowers, was the biggest tortoise they had ever seen. Much bigger than the two friends they had just met. She looked old and wise. Aaron and Derek knew they had nothing to fear.

"This is our Grandma and she will make sure you feel better in no time!" Toby exclaimed with a wide smile on his face.

Grandma Tortoise got up and examined Derek's injured wing carefully.

She muttered something to herself and slowly made her way to the numerous fruits growing in her burrow. She picked a few of them and started crushing them together in a beautiful, jewel-encrusted bowl. She kept muttering words to herself while doing it. The whole atmosphere felt very solemn. Everyone was as quiet as a mouse, intently watching every move Grandma Tortoise made.

Finally, Grandma Tortoise broke the silence and spoke for the first time, addressing Derek by saying, "I have made you a potion with juicy guavas, succulent mangoes and mouth-watering lychees. After you drink this, your wing will be mended, and you will be able to make your way back home again."

However, just before handing the potion to Derek, and while no one was looking, she secretly sprinkled a spoonful of magical herbs into it. Derek quickly gulped it down and every drop tasted heavenly. It was the most delicious drink he had ever had. Even before finishing the last drop, Derek could feel movement in his left wing again, and a few minutes later, he felt like his old self. He could flap his wing with absolutely no pain at all! Overjoyed, he gave the biggest hug to Tara, Toby and Grandma Tortoise.

Sharing stories of their previous adventures with their new found friends, Derek and Aaron soon realised it was time to leave. As the two friends started making their way out of the burrow, Grandma Tortoise stopped Derek to hand him something… a long, thin piece of a dazzling ruby-red precious stone.

"I can see that you are a dodo who loves going on exciting adventures, and sometimes along the way, trouble might find you. However, this precious stone will help you in more ways that you can imagine," whispered Grandma Tortoise gently into Derek's ear.

Tears of joy and gratitude filled Derek's

POST

eyes, and he hugged Grandma Tortoise one more time and thanked her for this priceless gift. Aaron and Derek then left the burrow, and to their surprise the cyclone was gone and the sky was once again bright blue. They waved goodbye to their new friends, and Derek soared higher and higher towards the beach, agreeing that maybe what they had been through was enough excitement for one day. However, as much as Derek wanted the day to end on a quiet note, that sadly would not be the case for him...

CHAPTER 6

The journey back was quite uneventful and exactly what the friends wanted after their lucky escape. As they touched down in front of Aaron's hut, they had never felt happier to be in such familiar surroundings again. They could taste the saltiness of the ocean and feel the warm sea breeze on their faces. This provided them with some much-needed comfort.

"Thank you for yet another adventure," whispered Aaron into Derek's ear as he hugged his friend tightly.

"I am glad we are both okay," replied Derek, with a bright smile on his face.

As Derek got ready to fly back to the jungle, something suddenly caught his eye. It was a ship docked on the shore in the distance. It was bigger than your average ones that usually sailed through the island's seas. Derek's interest was already piqued, and he decided to wander closer to inspect the ship.

"Come on Aaron, let's go!" yelled Derek as he sprinted ahead.

As the friends reached the ship, they were startled by two booming voices that came out from behind one of the tall filao trees. As they peeked around the trees, one of the men bellowed, "Good afternoon, I'm Ryan and this is Rowan. This is our ship and we are treasure hunters!"

They both had scruffy hair and bloodshot eyes. Ryan had a scar on his right cheek while Rowan had a long, dirty beard almost touching his chest. As Ryan approached Aaron and Derek, a wide smile appeared on his face. However, it was not a reassuring smile, as he barely had any teeth, and the ones he had were all rotten. Aaron took an instant dislike to him, but Derek seemed to be in awe of the

fact that he was a treasure hunter. Derek very quickly introduced himself and very proudly told the two men that he was the only dodo on the island who could fly.

"A dodo that can fly! Surely that's impossible?" chuckled Ryan.

Derek took great pleasure in proving Ryan wrong. He flapped his wings and started flying over the shocked faces of Ryan and Rowan. The two treasure hunters' mouths fell open with shock. They could not quite believe what they were seeing. As Derek touched down in front of them, they seemed even more eager to speak to him.

"I bet a lot of people will pay a lot of money to see a unique dodo like you," sneered Rowan.

Aaron did not trust him at all, but Derek was enjoying all the attention. Rowan whispered something quickly in Ryan's ear, and Aaron knew straight away that they were up to no good.

"Derek, would you like to come inside our ship and see some of the treasures we have collected so far on our journey?" coaxed Ryan.

Derek could not believe how lucky he was. This sounded like yet another adventure, and he replied with an immediate, "Yes please!"

CHAPTER 7

Feeling a mixture of excitement and nervousness, Derek took one last look at Aaron, and as he rushed onto the ship, he shouted, "I'll see you in a short while." Once onboard, Ryan and Rowan beckoned Derek to follow them to the end of a long, dark, winding corridor. Derek started to get an ominous feeling.

He immediately said to Rowan, "You know what? It's getting a bit late so I should probably get back to the jungle before it gets too dark for me to fly. Maybe I can see the treasures another day?"

A smirk spread across Rowan's face. "Don't be silly, Derek. This is the opportunity of a lifetime. Surely you know that you will never get a chance to see so many unique treasures again?" he replied with a meanness in his voice that Derek unfortunately didn't pick up on.

Cautiously walking down the corridor, Ryan directed Derek to enter the last room at the end. Derek knew he shouldn't have kept going, but his curiosity got the better of him, and he really wanted to see the treasures. Walking into the room, it was cold and nearly completely bare, except for a bird cage in one corner.

Immediately, Derek knew he was in trouble! There was not a single treasure in sight. So why did those two men want to bring him to this room? Derek very quickly got his answer as the door slammed shut behind him... BANG!

"That will teach you not to follow strangers to strange places, you silly bird. You fell for my trick Derek, and a dodo that can fly will be worth so much when we can finally sell you!" boomed Ryan, followed by the meanest cackle Derek had ever heard.

Terrified, Derek moved to the corner. As he got closer to the bird cage he started to hear lots of different tunes, each one more melodious than the one before. It was truly soothing to the ears. Looking closely, he could see a parakeet inside. Its body had velvety rich emerald-green feathers, and it had a flamboyant pink beak. In contrast, its wing feathers were a mixture of shimmering gold, vibrant fire orange and dazzling aquamarine blue. It was truly the most beautiful and magnificent bird Derek had ever seen, definitely one of a kind.

"That must be why the parakeet has been captured. Surely a parakeet this unique and exquisite looking will fetch a lot of money too?" Derek thought to himself.

Rowan suddenly shouted through the closed door, issuing this stern warning, "You two keep each other company until we have reached our destination and don't try anything or there will be serious consequences!"

Tears started streaming down Derek's face as he realised he would never see his family and Aaron again.

The parakeet suddenly gently spoke in a reassuring voice saying, "Don't be sad. Maybe together we can work out a way to escape."

"But we are locked in this room. There is no way we can get out," said Derek despondently.

"Do you think you might be able to get me out of this cage first? Do you have anything on you that might help?" the parakeet asked in a pleading voice.

Derek's face suddenly lit up. He remembered the piece of precious stone that Grandma Tortoise had given him. That might be sharp enough to saw through some of the bars of the cage. Derek was absolutely delighted when his idea worked.

The parakeet flew out of the cage, happily spreading its beautiful wings. It looked so happy to finally be out. After what felt like hours of flying, although in reality was only a few minutes, the parakeet touched down next to Derek.

"Sorry, I haven't introduced myself yet. My name is Priya and I am really glad you are here. Maybe now we can help each other out and find a way off this ship," she said as she extended a friendly wing to Derek.

"Hi, my name is Derek. You seem very chirpy for someone who is trapped on a ship," said Derek quite inquisitively.

"That is because I really believe we can escape!" Priya said enthusiastically.

Derek admired her optimism, but he certainly didn't feel the same way. Suddenly, Derek's thought was interrupted by a flash of lightning, followed by the deafening rumble of thunder. This felt very familiar now. He looked outside through the tiny window in their room and the sky was pitch black. Instantly, he knew that the cyclone was back, and they were in for a very rough ride.

CHAPTER 8

The ship started rocking uncontrollably, and both Derek and Priya found themselves on the floor upside down. They tried their hardest to get up, but to no avail. They could hear screaming coming from Rowan and Ryan. They knew that the ship was in real trouble! Suddenly, they could see water trickling from under the door of their room. They immediately knew that the ship was sinking and they needed to get out. Derek, usually not one to shy away from any challenges, remained frozen in fear at the scene that was unravelling in front of him.

The water had changed from a small trickle to a torrent, rapidly filling the tiny room that they were in. Seeing Derek frozen, Priya knew that she had to be the brave one if they had any chance of getting out. Suddenly, Priya's eyes started gleaming with excitement. Derek looked

at her with sheer confusion. Priya managed to pull herself up and helped Derek do the same.

"Derek, do you still have your precious stone? I think I have an idea on how to get us out of here," shouted Priya triumphantly.

Derek immediately pulled the long jewel out and handed it to his new-found friend.

"I am going to try and pick the lock on the door. This may be our only chance of surviving," said Priya.

"Have you done this before?" asked Derek with a worrying tone.

"No, never, but I have to try," answered Priya, trying to reassure him.

Her positivity and optimism worked like an absolute charm as she managed to pick the lock on her very first try.

When they opened the door, the corridor was filled with water a few feet deep. The ship was rapidly filling with water as well, and it was sinking at an alarming speed. As the friends tried to find their way off the ship, the two nasty men crossed their path. They were, of course, trying to escape as well.

"Where do you two think you are going?" growled Rowan as he grabbed Priya's wing.

Ryan on the other hand was trying his hardest to get to Derek, who was attempting to move further and further away from the two mean men. Luckily, as Ryan nearly got his dirty hands around Derek, a gush of water filled the corridor and knocked the two men onto the floor. Derek managed to hold on to a nearby door with one wing and grab Priya with the other. They quickly made their way towards the deck while Ryan and Rowan were still trapped inside the ship.

As the two friends made it outside, onto the deck, they knew there was only one thing for them to do… they had to jump.

"Derek, I don't think I can do it. The ocean is too deep and vast. I will get lost and drown," cried Priya in a desperate voice.

It was Derek's turn to be brave now and remind his friend about her own bravery.

"Priya, we are still alive because of your amazing idea to escape from the room. You saved both of us with your fantastic lockpicking skills," said Derek in an encouraging voice. "Now I need you to trust me and follow my lead. I need you to hop on my back," continued Derek with a smile on his face.

Priya did as she was told. Before she knew it, Derek had jumped from the deck and into the vast ocean, which was now more slate grey instead of its usual

turquoise blue colour.

That was absolutely perfect timing, because as soon as Derek did that, the ship started sinking below the ocean waves. As the two friends watched in horror at the scene unfolding in front of them, they could see the two mean treasure hunters floating away on debris from the ship. Each of them was desperately fighting one another to hang on to the little piece of floating wood. It was a rather funny scene. Derek and Priya were ecstatic to finally be rid of them. However, as they looked at the pelting rain and the vast ocean that lay ahead of them, they knew that the next journey was not going to be easy for them.

CHAPTER 9

The rain and heavy winds were coming down harder and harder, making it nearly impossible for Derek to keep swimming. His wings and feet were aching from the swimming, and his eyes were stinging from the pelting rain. Although he was feeling very defeated by then, he certainly did not let Priya see this. He needed to stay positive for her, like she did for him when on the ship.

"Don't worry Priya, we are nearly there," shouted Derek in a convincing way, even though he knew they were nowhere near land.

After a while, Derek started to feel faint and thought he was hallucinating when he heard his name being shouted in the distance.

"DEREK, DON'T WORRY, WE ARE

COMING FOR YOU!" screamed a familiar voice.

Derek thought he must be hearing things, but the voice kept getting closer and closer. Finally, Derek turned round and if he had more energy, he would have jumped out of the water in joy at the unexpected sight in front of him. Approaching him was his best friend Aaron, sitting on top of a dolphin. As Aaron got closer to Derek, he swiftly helped both Derek and Priya out of the stormy water and safely onto the dolphin's back.

"How did you know to come find me?" shouted Derek with tears of joy.

"As soon as I saw the ship setting sail, I knew you were in trouble, and I never liked the look of those two mean men," replied Aaron.

Aaron further explained how he had asked for help from Dolly the Dolphin to rescue his friend, and she had been more than happy to oblige.

With all three friends grabbing on for dear life, Dolly swam effortlessly, even in the torrential rain and heavy wind. Soon they could see the shore coming into view, and soon after, the rain calmed down. The grey sky was slowly replaced by a clear blue sky again.

As the four friends finally made it back to the white sandy beach, the sun was now shining brightly again. Everything felt just right. A wave of relief swept over Derek. There were times on the ship when Derek did not think he would ever be back here again. All three friends thanked Dolly wholeheartedly for getting them back to safety as they relaxed on the warm sand. Suddenly, Aaron dashed off in the direction of his hut. A few minutes later, he reappeared holding some big coconuts.

"I thought we could all do with a refreshing drink after our exhausting

journey back!" exclaimed Aaron happily.

The friends slowly sipped their drinks while Derek and Priya started relating their challenging and frightening adventure on the ship. Aaron and Dolly listened in horror, but at the same time, they were in awe at the braveness of their friends. By the time they were done with their story, the sun was setting on the horizon. Both Derek and Priya realised it was time to go home.

Priya had not seen her family in a long time after being captured, and Derek was just as keen to get back to the jungle and his family. They both promised to see each other again and who knows, have one or two more adventures along the way too. Waving goodbye to Aaron and Dolly, Derek and Priya were both soon flying high in the sky in opposite directions towards the loving arms of their families.

Despite feeling the weight of his achy wings, Derek reached the jungle in no time and was bursting with happiness at the sight of Mummy Dodo, Daddy Dodo and Grandad Dodo. As usual his family welcomed him back, beaming with excitement.

Derek recounted what had happened during the day to his family. They too were shocked to hear that they had nearly lost him to the cyclone, those two mean men, and a sinking ship. Derek promised to be more careful on his next adventure, although whether this would happen still remained to be seen!

Finally, tired and aching all over, Derek managed to drag himself to bed that night, ecstatic at yet another thrilling adventure. As he started to fall asleep, he thanked the lucky shooting star once again for giving him the ability to fly, discover the wonders of this amazing island, and make new friends.

He was certainly the luckiest dodo alive!